Introduction to the 2024 Edition

Specimens of New Process Wood Type! was issued by the William H. Page Wood Type Company in 1890. There are three copies known to exist, according to scholar David Shields, author of *The Rob Roy Kelly Wood Type Collection: A History and Catalog.* The copy at Columbia University includes the printed date of January 1890, and came to Columbia from Hamilton Manufacturing Company in 1961 via Rob Roy Kelly. The copies at Rochester Institute of Technology and the Newberry Library are dated to May 1890 according to Shields, and were printed for Page's distributor Dauchy & Co. of New York. Aside from minor differences in the front matter and covers, the specimens shown are identical. The two different covers of these copies are shown on the back cover of this edition.

This new facsimile edition was created at the suggestion of John Horn, from Shooting Star Press, who is a collector of wood type and specimens. He was aware that this is the only source of information to identify Page die-cut wood types, and he had obtained a copy of this catalog in a facsimile edition published by American Life Foundation in 1983 as *Late Victorian Wood Types, Borders, and Ornaments.* This little-known publisher also issued a number of reprints of nineteenth century architectural volumes. One critic who admired some of their work also commented, "More annoying is the publisher's habit of giving new titles to old works, a practice that is sure to cause confusion for historians and librarians alike." Their reprint of the Page specimen is scarce in libraries and extremely scarce in the used book market.

Late Victorian Wood Types, Borders, and Ornaments.

THE AMERICAN LIFE FOUNDATION is a non-profit, educational institution specializing in the acquisition and dissemination of knowledge through publications. Open to the study of all aspects of American life, it is especially interested in the relationships of things and ideas and how the social functions of artifacts from the past relate to those of today. Recently, it has been republishing many nineteenth-century stylebooks about architecture and the decorative arts to assist old house owners and other preservationists. For a free listing write:

American Life Books, Box 349, Watkins Glen, NY 14891.
ISBN: 0-89257-056-3

This edition was scanned from John Horn's facsimile copy, so the quality of some of the thinner type such as running heads, page numbers, and type name labels is less than optimal, but largely still legible. Significant efforts have been made to optimize the print quality for this new facsimile, but defects remain that we hope will not detract from the new availability of otherwise almost unobtainable specimens.

William Page and his company had first introduced die-cut wood borders in 1879. He extended this process to wood type in the late 1880s as documented in a series of patents filed in 1887, 1888, and 1889. In the successive patents the process progressed from combining pantograph and die-cutting, to whole-letter dies, and then to modular dies that employed several dies in succession to form the parts of each letter. The modular approach required fewer dies, so that for example the left curve could be used for a "C" or "O", and another die could be used for the left side of a "B" or "D" and many other characters.

The development of "new process wood type" was a response to competition from J. E. Hamilton's veneer Holly Wood Type, which was sold at a much lower cost than Page's traditional wood type cut by pantograph in end-grain maple. The die-cut process was competitive with Hamilton's product because it was able to produce type at a much lower cost and in much less time than the pantograph method, but it was limited to the exact sizes and styles of the expensive dies that were required.

The "new process" proved to be short lived, because one year after this specimen was published William Page sold his wood type company to Hamilton in 1891. Hamilton incorporated all of Page's designs and equipment, and continued to advertise die-cut type until 1906.

Hamilton also continued to make die-cut borders using Page's equipment and dies into the 1940s. In recent years the Hamilton Wood Type and Printing Museum has revived the process of creating new die-cut borders, thanks to the efforts of industrial archaeologist Daniel Schneider. At the time there were no living former employees of Hamilton who knew how the border stamping equipment worked, so Daniel reverse-engineered the process based on the surviving equipment. Referencing examples of old stamped borders and existing dies, he worked out the process of dies that were stamped in step-and-repeat sequence to create each design. The museum is now able to demonstrate the stamping equipment and create new borders for sale in limited quantities.

The equipment and dies for the "new process" wood type shown in this specimen are not known to survive, so mystery shrouds some details.

— *Matthew Kelsey, Liber Apertus Press*

PAGE'S NEW PROCESS

WOOD TYPE!

Equal to the best Cut Type at a fraction of the price.

A REVOLUTION IN WOOD TYPE MAKING

This Type is made of SOLID ROCK MAPLE, finished exactly the same, in every respect, as our well known machine cut wood type, the only difference being that the face is cut on the wood by dies, by Wm. H. Page's New Patent Process, instead of the expensive old pantagraph machine method.

Wood Borders and Ornaments have been made by this new method for nearly ten years, but it is only lately that the invention of machinery has made it possible to apply it to the making of Wood Type. The face of the New Process Type is much more perfect and clear cut than was possible to produce by the old method, as the dies now finish each letter without any hand trimming.

Thousands of fonts of this New Process Type have already been sold. It is used in every state in the Union and in Canada, and it gives satisfaction everywhere. Printers have used the New Process Ornaments and Borders for ten years with satisfaction, and they find that the New Process Letter works like them in every particular.

Examine the price list herewith and see that this Solid Rock Maple Type can be bought for less money than any of the veneered or skim-coated stuff now on the market, and there is no neccessity of the printers having to put up with poor substitutes for genuine Wood Type in order to make a temporary saving. We do not have to advertise that "the face of this type will never come off" as each letter is a solid maple block, and we guarantee it to wear as well as any type we ever made. The Wm. H. Page Wood Type Company's Wood Type has for years been the standard of excellence the world over.

Mr. Page the inventor of this New Process Type has made it possible for every printer to add a poster printing department to his establishment at so small an outlay, that he can work it profitably. In smaller sizes this new type will take the place of metal letter, as it is very much cheaper and much more durable, besides being lighter and much easier to handle.

The New Wood Type is *ONLY MADE IN THE SIZES SHOWN* in the specimens, but new styles and sizes are being constantly added.

THE WM. H. PAGE WOOD TYPE COMPANY,

NORWICH,

CONN.

TESTIMONIALS.

We have hundreds of letters from printers all over the country congratulating us on producing such splendid type at so low a price and pronouncing it thoroughly satisfactory and equal to any they have ever used. We have been making New Process Type for over two years now and are satisfied that it is a success and are willing to send it out under our name and recommend it, without fear that our thirty years reputation as the first house in wood type manufacturing, will suffer.

READ THESE DIRECTIONS

BEFORE ORDERING

NEW PROCESS TYPE.

First; do not order any size not shown in this book, as no other sizes are made.

Second; be particular to specify how **many A's are** wanted for a font and whether the lower case and figures are wanted, and give the *size* or number of lines pica Carelessness in this matter keeps us writing letters to find out these little points and is the cause, many times, of great delay in filling orders.

And NOTE That

We expect to keep in stock all the styles and sizes shown in this book and can fill orders promptly, and we have made arrangements to keep a complete stock of this type at Chicago and San Francisco.

It is expected that large orders will be filled at the factory as well as the ordinary machine cut type.

We do not make any of the old faces by this process at present, these faces are all new, but we can make larger sizes of any styles shown in this book by the old machine cut processs.

New Process Type like all other wood type should not be *soaked* in water, but the ink simply wiped off the face before it has had time to dry on. Cotton waste moistened with benzine is the best for this purpose, although water or lye will not effect it unless the type is soaked, which would injure any wood type ever made. In short the New Process Type should be treated just the same as any careful printer would use any other wood type. It is in no way inferior to the best type ever made by us by our old method and just as durable.

SCALE OF FONTS.

3A Capitals.		3a L'r. Case.		4A Capitals.		4a L'r. Case.		5A Capitals		5a L'r. Case.	
75 LETTERS.		65 LETTERS.		106 LETTERS.		90 LETTERS.		120 LETTERS.		104 LETTERS.	
A	3	a	3	A	4	a	4	A	5	a	5
B	2	b	2	B	3	b	3	B	3	b	3
C	2	c	2	C	3	c	3	C	4	c	4
D	2	d	2	D	3	d	3	D	4	d	4
E	4	e	4	E	5	e	5	E	6	e	6
F	2	f	2	F	3	f	3	F	3	f	3
G	2	g	2	G	3	g	3	G	3	g	3
H	2	h	2	H	3	h	3	H	4	h	4
I	4	i	3	I	4	i	4	I	5	i	5
J	2	j	1	J	3	j	2	J	3	j	2
K	1	k	1	K	2	k	2	K	2	k	2
L	4	l	4	L	5	l	5	L	6	l	6
M	2	m	2	M	3	m	3	M	4	m	4
N	3	n	3	N	4	n	4	N	5	n	5
O	3	o	3	O	4	o	4	O	5	o	5
P	2	p	2	P	3	p	3	P	3	p	3
Q	1	q	1	Q	2	q	2	Q	2	q	2
R	3	r	3	R	4	r	4	R	5	r	5
S	4	s	4	S	5	s	5	S	6	s	6
T	3	t	4	T	4	t	4	T	5	t	5
U	2	u	2	U	3	u	3	U	4	u	4
V	2	v	2	V	3	v	3	V	3	v	3
W	2	w	2	W	3	w	3	W	3	w	3
X	1	x	1	X	2	x	2	X	2	x	2
Y	2	y	2	Y	3	y	3	Y	3	y	3
Z	1	z	1	Z	2	z	2	Z	2	z	2
&	1	fi	1	&	2	fi	1	&	2	fi	1
!	2	fl	1	!	3	fl	1	!	3	fl	1
.	3	ff	1	.	4	ff	1	.	4	ff	1
-	1	ffi	1	-	1	ffi	1	-	1	ffi	1
,	2	ffl	1	,	2	ffl	1	,	2	ffl	1
:	1			:	2			:	2		
;	1			;	2			;	2		
,	3			,	4			,	4		

Figures,	1	2	3	4	5	6	7	8	9	0	$	
No. of each,	3	2	2	2	2	2	2	3	2	5	1	26

BORDERS PER FOOT.

No 150 to	Cts	No.	Cts	No.	Cts	No	Cts
194	40	217	1,20	221¾	75	312	30
195	30	218	1,20	205½	75	313	40
196	30	219	1,20	268	40	314	40
197	30	220	75	269	75	315	40
198	30	221	75	270	75	316	40
199	30	222	40	271	75	317	40
200	1,20	223	40	272	75	318	50
201	1,20	224	40	273	40	319	40
202	1,20	225	40	274	50	320	50
203	60	227	75	275	1 20	321	50
204	30	228	40	276	40	322	60
205	60	229	1,20	277	40	323	75
206	60	232	2,00	278	40	324	75
207	60	233	75	279	40	325	60
208	40	234	75	280	60	326	75
209	30	235	1,20	281	60	327	70
210	30	239	75	282	60	328	75
211	30	240	75	283	75	329	70
212	30	241	75	284	75	330	50
213	40	242	40	285	60	331	40
214	70	243	40	286	60	332	50
215	70	244	40	287	60		
216	1,20	245	30	288	75		
		246	30	289	75		
		247	30	290	75		
		248	30	291	75		
		249	30	292	75		
		250	40	293	40		
		251	40	294	30		
		252	40	295	30		
		253	40	296	30		
		254	40	297	30		
		255	60	298	30		
		256	75	299	30		
		257	60	300	60		
		258	1,20	301	60		
		259	40	302	60		
		260	40	303	60		
		261	75	304	75		
		263	1,50	305	60		
		203½	60	306	75		
		251½	40	307	60		
		262½	40	308 1-2	40		
		262¾	40	309	40		
		266½	1.00	310	60		
		221½	75				

Space Ornaments, PER PAIR.

5 line 15 cents,
6 line 17 cents,
7 line 20 cents,
8 line 22 cents,
10 line 25 cents.

Six Line Border No. 511, 60 cents per foot.
Six Line Border No. 512, 50 cents per foot.
Seven Line Border No. 512, 50 cents per foot
Eight Line Border No. 512, 60 cents per foot.
Ten Line Border No 512, 75 cents per foot.
Six Line Border No. 513, 60 cents per foot.
Seven Line Border No. 513, 60 cents per foot.
Eleven Line Border No. 513, 75 cents per foot.

PRICE LIST

OF OUR

NEW PROCESS TYPE.

LINES PICA	CLASS M CENTS	CLASS N CENTS	CLASS O CENTS	CLASS P CENTS
2	2	2 1-4	2 1-2	3
3	2 1-4	2 1-2	3	3 1-2
4	2 1-2	3	3 1-4	4
5	3	3 1-2	4	4 1-2
6	3 1-2	4	4 1-2	5 1-2
7	4	4 1-2	5	6
8	4 1-2	5	5 1-2	6 1-2
10	5	5 1-2	6	7
12	5 1-2	6	6 1-2	7 1-2
15	6	6 1-2	7	8
18	7	7 1-2	8	9

150

151

152

153

154

155

156

157

158

159

160

161

162

163

164

165

166

167

168

169

170

171

172

173

174

175

176

177

178

179

180

181

182

183

184

185

186

187

188

189

190

191

192

193

195

196

197

198

199

204

206

207

208

209

210

211

220

222

223

224

225

227

228

233

239

240

243

245

246

247

248

249

250

252

253

254

255

256

257

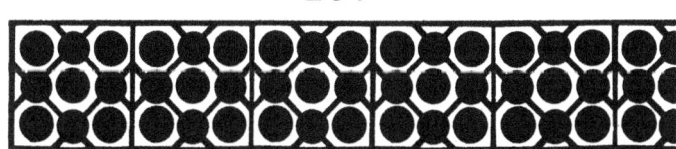

258

259

260

261

203 1–2

251 1-2

221 1-2

221 3-4

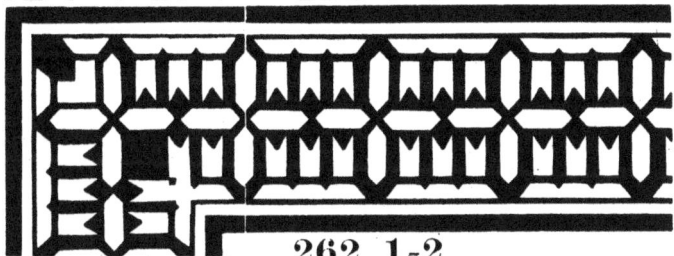

262 1-2

262 3-4

266 1-2

271

272

273

274

276

277

279

280

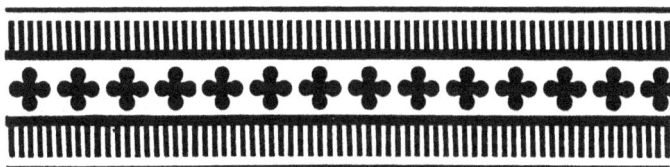

281

282

205 1-2

268

269

270

283

284

285

286

287

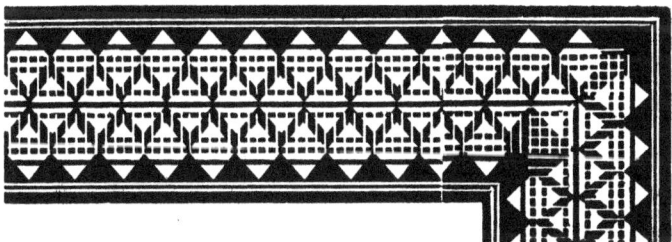

288

289

290

291

292

293

294

295

296

297

298

299

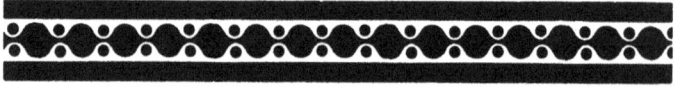

300

301

302

303

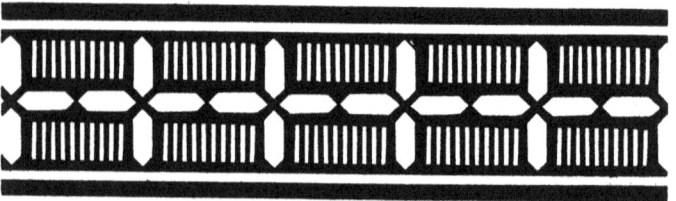

304

305

306

307

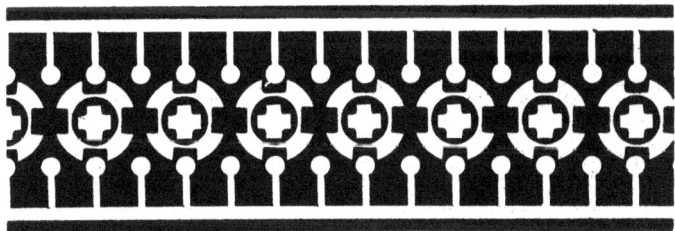

319

320

321

322

323

324

325

326

327

328

329

312

313

314

315

316

317

318

511

512   *SIX LINE*

512   *SEVEN LINE*

512   *EIGHT LINE*

512   *TEN LINE*

Six Line Border No. 512.

Seven Line Border No. 512.

Eleven Line Border No. 512.

Five Line Space Ornaments.

400 **404**

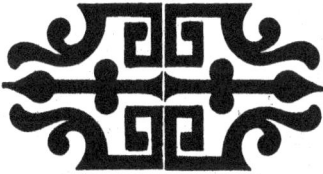 

409 **407** **406**

403 **402**

410 **408** **410**

401 **405**

 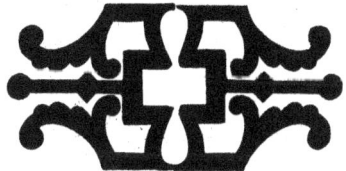

Seven Line Space Ornaments. **402**   **403**

401

407

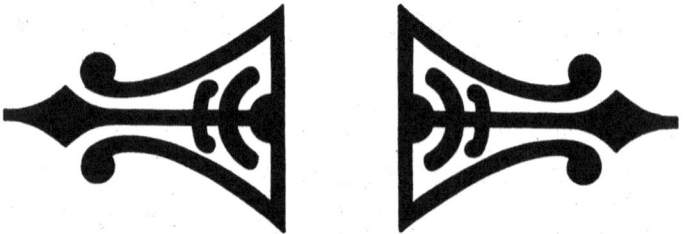

409

Seven Line Space Ornaments.   **404**

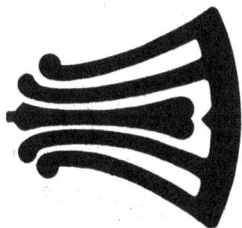 

408

400

Eight Line Space Ornaments.   **405**

Six Line Space Ornaments.

406 **407** **410**

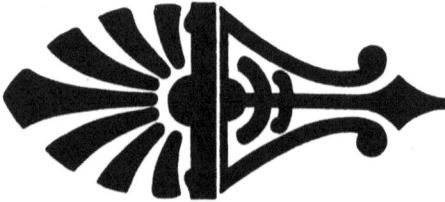 

409 **408**

403 **404** **405**

400 **402** **401**

Ten Line Space Ornaments.

400

404

330

405

401

331

Eight Line Space Ornaments.

410

401

404

Ten Line Space Ornaments.

407

409

330

406

410

Four Line 500.   Class N

IMPROVISERS
Tonsorials $44

Ten Line 500.   N

STAR
Man13

Five Line 500.   Class N

MANCHETS

Juvenile 839

Eight Line 500.   N

ROWIN

Prices31

Six Line 500.   Class N

NORWICH

Twelve Line 500.   N

BIRD

Nest4

Seven Line 500.   Class N

SMOKE!

Aldine 74

Fifteen Line 500.   N

PEG

Six Line 500.   Class N

Condensed I

Eight Line 501.   M

BUGERS 143

Ten Line 501.   M

DIXEYS 71

Ten Line 502.   Class N

GROWN 7

Twelve Line 502.   N

QUIT 43

Six Line 503.   N

EXCRESCENCES

Six Line 503.   Class N

Personators 44

Ten Line 503.   N

STOCKNG

Beans 167

Seven Line 503. Class N

ARCHITECTS

Modern $355

Twelve Line 503. N

STORES

Fifteen Line 503.   Class N

COUGH

Soda 13

Eight Line 503.   Class N

MEASURES

Patches $13

Twelve Line 503.   N

Maid 25

Three Line 504.   Class P

GLORIOUS !

Common 48

Ten Line 504.   P

GIT

Se7

Five Line 504. Class P

TEARS

Men 41

Eight Line 504. P

MIX

Bef 3

Four Line 504.   Class P

RAVINE!

Golden 19

Six Line 504.   P

OPRA

End 5

Seven Line 504.   P

LINE

Seven Line 504.   Class P

Sub l

Twelve Line 504.   P

NG
Cot

Three Line 505.   Class P

HUDSON 1651

Four Line 505.   P

FORM $42

Five Line 505.   P

CART 32

Six Line 505.   P

MUGS 5

Seven Line 505.   P

FOR 15

Eight Line 505.   Class P

HOE7

Ten Line 505.   P

MUG

Twelve Line 505.   P

BIT

Four and one-half Line 506.   Class N

Borders 1239

Four Line 506.   N

MAJORITIES !

Solomonize 69

Eight Line 506.   N

SAUCE!

Meat 18

Four and one-half Line 506.   Class N

WONDERFIT

Twelve Line 506.   N

VINE
Finel

Six Line 506.　　　　Class N

TENTION!

March 46

Seven Line 506.　　　　N

BOTHER

Some315

Five Line 506.   Class N

ORNAMEN !

Secures 84i

Ten Line 506.   N

MORT

For 25

Fifteen Line 506.   Class N

CEN

Wel

Three Line 507.   Class P

FURNITURE
Parlor Set 18

Four Line 507.   P

LONGNIR
Luxures 5

Eight Line 507.   P

RUM
Git13

Six Line 508. Class P

BRINE
Pork 5

Seven Line 508. P

LONE
Mac 3

Five Line 507. Class P

MAKE!
Fun 512

Ten Line 507. P

BIT
Ribl

Two Line 507.   Class P

MUNIFICENT GIFT
Auction Sale At 4

Twelve Line 507.   P

MC
In5

Fifteen Line 507.   Class P

CO
hn1

Six Line 507.   Class P

HUNCH

Groan7

Seven Line 507.   P

ROME

Boil 71

Four Line 508. Class P

TIGHT MID
Governor 1

Ten Line 508. P

GEO
To 5

Five Line 508.   Class P

SENDER

Union 58

Eight Line 508.   P

TINE

Men 1

Three Line 508   Class P

HOLDFASTER
Glorios Era 18

Twelve Line 508.   P

CIP
Lo7

Fifteen Line 508.   Class P

NU
Sic

Four Line 509. Class O

MINORITIES

Wonderful 8

Eight Line 509. O

THUM

Cars 8

Six Line 509.   Class O

BOSTON
Elms 56

Seven Line 509.   O

BUNCH
Rats 14

Three Line 509. Class O

COUNT NEANCE
Felonious $8138

Twelve Line 509. O

SON
Vin1

Five Line 509. Class O

NUETERN

World 158

Ten Line 509 O

NUM

Mo 21

Fifteen Line 509. Class O

ISH

Pel

Three Line 510.   Class O

MAKE STAMP TYPE
Attachments 6785

Twelve Line 510.   O

SHEP
Com l

Five Line 510.   Class O

TEN MANT

Swarms 392

Eight Line 510.   O

GEORGE

Urn $33

Four Line 510.   Class O

FROZEN VINES

General Notion

Ten Line 510.   Class O

SNOW

But 48

Six Line 510. Class O

MANSION
Great $38

Seven Line 510. O

RONNON
Tubbs 13

Fifteen Line 510.   Class O

PUT

Frel

Six Line 511.   Class N

EGYPTION !

Mineral $8

Seven Line 511.   N

SPECIMEN

Minder 23

Five Line 511.   Class N

BLACK TANKS

Founder 258

Eight Line 511.   N

HOTHOM

Irons 56

Four Line 511   Class N

HANGGINGARDEN

Ten Line 511.   N

MVRCH

Tom33

Four Line 511.   Class N

Snowclod Mount

Twelve Line 511.   N

GIRLS
Rut 18

Fifteen Line 511.   Class N

MAN

Fur 8

Five Line 512.　　　Class N

ORTHOGRAPHIC

Editorials 8546

Eight Line 512.　　　N

SAW MILL

Pianas 38

Six Line 512.   Class N

STAMP TYPE

Makers 923

Seven Line 512.   N

COLLECTOR

Pinched 78

Four Line 512.   Class N

NEW PROCESS TYPE

Ten Line 512.   N

HORNED
Pine 45

Four Line 512. Class N

Musical Mirth 953

Twelve Line 512. N

LUNCH
Leaf 51

Fifteen Line 513.   Class M

PEAR

Tom5

Six Line 513.   Class M

CAPTALIZATION !

Reflections $53

Eight Line 513.   M

PHOTOGRAPH

Freddie 243

Five Line 513. M

TEMPESTUOUSNESS!

Hurricane sure 853

Ten Line 513. Class M

KINDLINDG

Diser 423

Fifteen Line 513.   Class M

HARAK

Hand 21

Seven Line 513.   Class M

NEW STYLSEN

Twelve Line 513.   M

MERBLER

Palaces 1

Seven Line 513. Class M

We Usefull 124

Ten Line 514. O

QIN

Cete

Fifteen Line 514.   Class O

SY

JK

Twelve Line 515.   Class N

BEC

Fifteen Line 515.   N

SIE

Twelve Line 516.   Class N

TRUE

Fifteen Line 516.   N

MIN

Twelve Line 514.   Class O

Ten Line 515.   N

Ten Line 516.   N

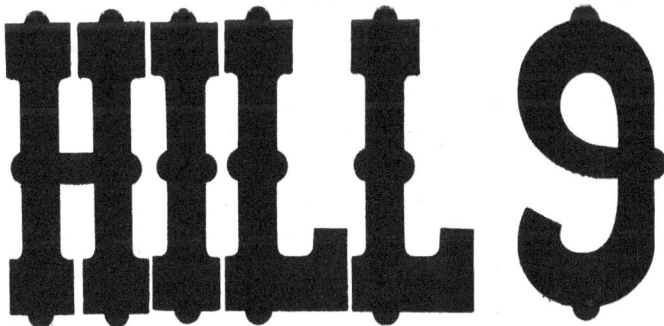

Eight Line 514.   Class O

MEN
Son8

Eight Line 515.   N

HOOD

www.ingramcontent.com/pod-product-compliance
Lightning Source LLC
Chambersburg PA
CBHW050844270326
41930CB00020B/3473